Nelson Literacy

Senior Author
Jennette MacKenzie

Senior Consultant
Miriam P. Trehearne

Senior Consultant
Carmel Crévola

Series Consultants
Ruth McQuirter Scott—*Word Study*
Mary Reid—*Assessment*
Steven Reid—*Assessment*
James Coulter—*Assessment*
Neil Andersen—*Media*
Maureen Innes—*ESL/ELL*
Rod Peturson—*Science*
Maurice De Giuseppe—*Science*
Nancy Christoffer—*Bias and Equity*

Series Writing Team
Paula S. Goepfert, *Senior Writer*

Marg Camp
Kathleen Corrigan
James Coulter
Dianne Dillabough
Lalie Harcourt
Jane Hutchison
Karen Kahler
Norma Kennedy
Christel Kleitsch

Wendy Mathieu
Christine McClymont
Heather McGowan
Bev McMorris
Thérèse McNamara
Sarah Peterson
Liz Powell
Mary Schoones
Ricki Wortzman

NELSON EDUCATION

NELSON EDUCATION

Nelson Literacy 3c
Jennette MacKenzie

Director of Publishing
Kevin Martindale

**General Manager,
Literacy and Reference**
Michelle Kelly

Director of Publishing, Literacy
Joe Banel

Publisher, Literacy
Rivka Cranley

**Managing Editor,
Development**
Lara Caplan

Senior Product Manager
Mark Cressman

Program Manager
Tracey MacDonald

Developmental Editors
Tara Harte
Norma Kennedy
David MacDonald

Researchers
Jane Hutchison
Dianne Dillabough

Editorial Assistants
Meghan Newton
Kendel Doyle

**Director, Content and Media
Production**
Carol Martin

Content Production Editor
Natalie Russell

Copy Editor
Linda Jenkins

Proofreader
Linda Szostak

Production Manager
Helen Locsin

Production Coordinator
Vicki Black

**Director, Asset Management
Services**
Vicki Gould

Design Director
Ken Phipps

Managing Designer
Sasha Moroz

Series Design
Sasha Moroz

Series Wordmark
Sasha Moroz
Steven Savicky

Cover Design
Sasha Moroz
Courtney Hellam

Interior Design
Carianne Bauldry
Jarrel Breckon
Courtney Hellam
InContext Publishing Partners
Jennifer Laing
Jennifer Leung
Sasha Moroz
Jan John Rivera

Asset Coordinators
Suzanne Peden
Renée Ford

Compositor
Courtney Hellam

Photo Research and Permissions
Natalie Barrington

Printer
Transcontinental Printing

COPYRIGHT © 2009 by Nelson
Education Ltd.

ISBN-13: 978-0-17-633251-8
ISBN-10: 0-17-633251-0

Printed and bound in Canada
6 7 12 11

For more information contact
Nelson Education Ltd.,
1120 Birchmount Road, Toronto,
Ontario, M1K 5G4. Or you can visit
our Internet site.

Every effort has been made to
trace ownership of all copyrighted
material and to secure permission
from copyright holders. In the
event of any question arising as
to the use of any material, we will
be pleased to make the necessary
corrections in future printings.

Advisers and Reviewers: Ontario

Nora Alexander

Stephanie Aubertin, Limestone DSB

Gale Bankowski, Hamilton-Wentworth CDSB

Wendy Bedford, Peterborough Victoria Northumberland and Clarington CDSB

Trudy Bell, Grand Erie DSB

Debra Boddy, Toronto DSB

Maggie Boss, Dufferin-Peel CDSB

Michelle Bryden, Eastern Ontario CDSB

Elizabeth M. Burchat, Renfrew CDSB

Karen Byromshaw, Toronto DSB

Mary Cairo, Toronto CDSB

Cheryl Chapman, Avon Maitland DSB

Cathy Chaput, Wellington CDSB

Christina Clancy, Dufferin-Peel CDSB

Alison Cooke, Grand Erie DSB

Sue Coutts, Simcoe County DSB

Cheryl Cristobal, Dufferin-Peel CDSB

Genevieve Dowson, Hamilton-Wentworth CDSB

Denise Edwards, Toronto DSB

Ted Gibb, Thames Valley DSB and University of Western Ontario

Lorraine Giroux, District School Board of Niagara

Charmaine Graves, Thames Valley DSB

Angela Harrison, York Region DSB

Colleen Hayward, Toronto CDSB

Charmaine Hung, Toronto DSB

Eddie Ing, Toronto DSB

Sue Jackson, Thames Valley DSB

Lee Jones-Imhotep, Toronto DSB

Ray King, Dufferin-Peel CDSB

Tanya Korostil, Peel DSB

Luci Lackey, Upper Grand DSB

Rocky Landon, Limestone DSB

Helen Lavigne, Waterloo CDSB

Laurie Light, Dufferin-Peel CDSB

Lorrie Lowes, Ottawa-Carleton DSB

Maria Makuch, Ottawa-Carleton DSB

Jennifer Mandarino, Dufferin-Peel CDSB

Carolyn March, Hamilton-Wentworth DSB

Mary Marshall, Halton DSB

Claire McDowell, Lambton Kent DSB

Thérèse McNamara, Simcoe County DSB

Andrew Mildenberger, Toronto DSB

Shirley Moorman, Simcoe County DSB

Laura Mossey, Durham DSB

Elisena Mycroft, Hamilton-Wentworth DSB

Mary Anne Olah, Toronto DSB

Judy Onody, Toronto CDSB

Eleanor Pardoe, Grand Erie DSB

Krista Pedersen, Upper Grand DSB

Sarah Peterson, Waterloo DSB

Annemarie Petrasek, Huron Perth CDSB

Catherine Pollock, Toronto DSB

Cheryl Potvin, Ottawa-Carleton DSB

Amarjit Rai, Peel DSB

Tara Rajaram-Donaldson, Toronto DSB

Mary Reid, Bluewater DSB

Kelly Rilley, Windsor-Essex CDSB

Joanne Saragosa, Toronto CDSB

Katherine Shaw, Peel DSB

Jackie Stafford, Toronto DSB

Elizabeth Taylor, Peel DSB

Sian Thomas, Renfrew DSB

Elizabeth Thompson, Durham DSB

Bonnie Tkac-Feetham, Niagara CDSB

Sandra VandeCamp, Dufferin-Peel CDSB

Ann Varty, Trillium Lakelands DSB

Contents

Welcome to Nelson Literacy

Your *Nelson Literacy* book is full of fascinating stories and articles. Many of the topics are the same as those you will study in science, social studies, and health.

Here are the different kinds of pages you will see in this book:

Let's Talk

Here's a chance to have some fun and also show what you know.

Understanding Strategies

These pages introduce you to reading, writing, speaking, listening, and media literacy strategies. Some pages have sticky notes with hints about the strategies.

Applying Strategies

These pages give you the chance to try out the strategies you've learned.

Putting It All Together

At the end of each unit, you'll have the chance to use the strategies that you've learned.

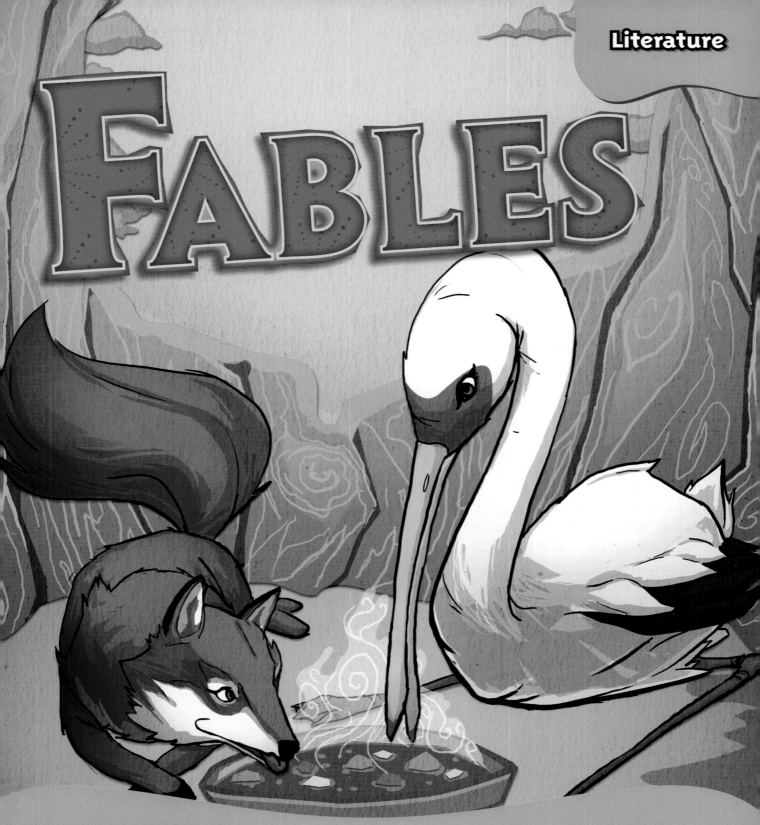

FABLES

In this unit, you will

- identify characteristics of fables
- combine sentences in your writing
- retell stories
- express opinions about illustrations
- use tone and volume while speaking

Tell the Fable

These illustrations are from the fable "The Lion and the Mouse," but they're mixed up! Talk about what is happening in each picture. Figure out the order of the events. Then tell the fable.

Narrative: Identifying Characteristics of Fables

Fables have certain characteristics that make them fables:

- The characters in fables are often animals.

- All the events connect to the problem at the beginning of the fable.

- The characters are usually very clever or very foolish.

- Fables teach a lesson, which is often called the "moral."

All the events connect to the problem at the beginning of the fable. What is the problem at the beginning of this fable?

The characters in fables are often animals. What animal characters are in this story?

Rabbit Tricks Elephant and Whale

An African fable retold by Banji Chikezie
Illustrated by Andy Elkerton

One day in the jungle, Elephant passed Rabbit. "How are you doing, Elephant?" asked Rabbit politely.

Elephant looked down his trunk and snorted, "Hop away, little Rabbit! I don't talk to anyone as small as you."

Rabbit was shocked to be talked to that way. She was so hurt by Elephant's rudeness that she hopped away without saying a word.

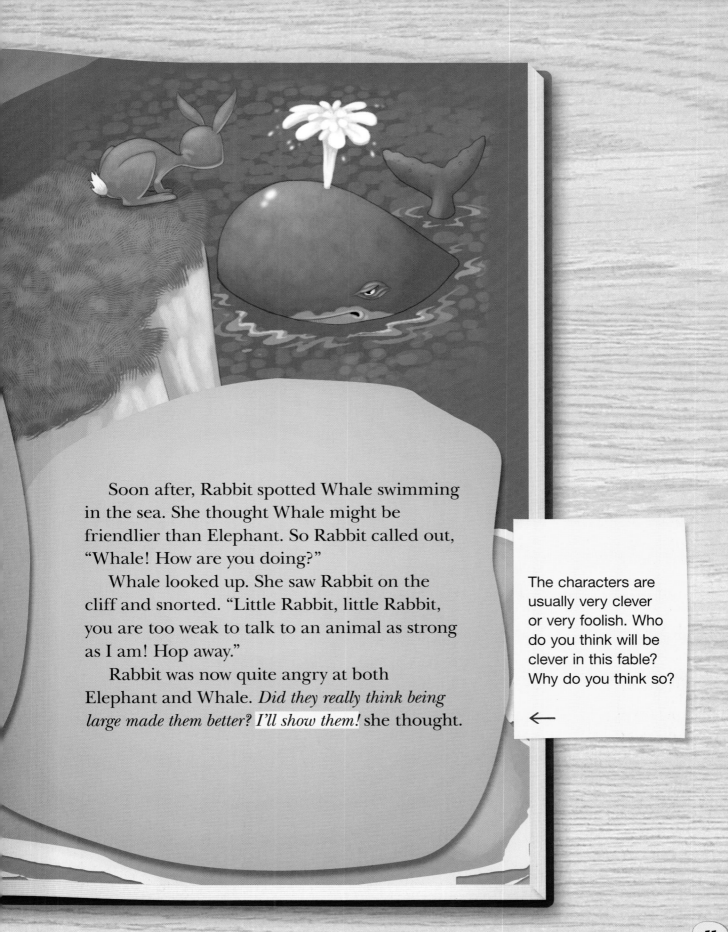

Soon after, Rabbit spotted Whale swimming in the sea. She thought Whale might be friendlier than Elephant. So Rabbit called out, "Whale! How are you doing?"

Whale looked up. She saw Rabbit on the cliff and snorted. "Little Rabbit, little Rabbit, you are too weak to talk to an animal as strong as I am! Hop away."

Rabbit was now quite angry at both Elephant and Whale. *Did they really think being large made them better?* I'll show them! she thought.

The characters are usually very clever or very foolish. Who do you think will be clever in this fable? Why do you think so?

←

Rabbit called out, "Whale! I can prove I am stronger than you! Which of us do you think will win a game of Tug-of-War?"

Whale laughed so hard she snorted water from her blowhole. "Little Rabbit, little Rabbit, don't be so foolish. You know I must win! Get a rope and I'll show you."

Rabbit hopped away to look for a thick, strong vine. After finding it, she went to find Elephant. "Elephant," she said, "this morning you were so rude to me! You think because I'm small I'm not as strong as you. Do you think you can beat me at Tug-of-War?"

Elephant roared with laughter. "Little Rabbit, you are foolish to challenge me. Give me that rope." Elephant tied the rope around his waist.

"Wait here, Elephant. I need room to pull you. When I yell 'pull,' you pull as hard as you can! I don't think you'll be able to move me."

All the events connect to the problem at the beginning of the fable. Why does Rabbit challenge Elephant?

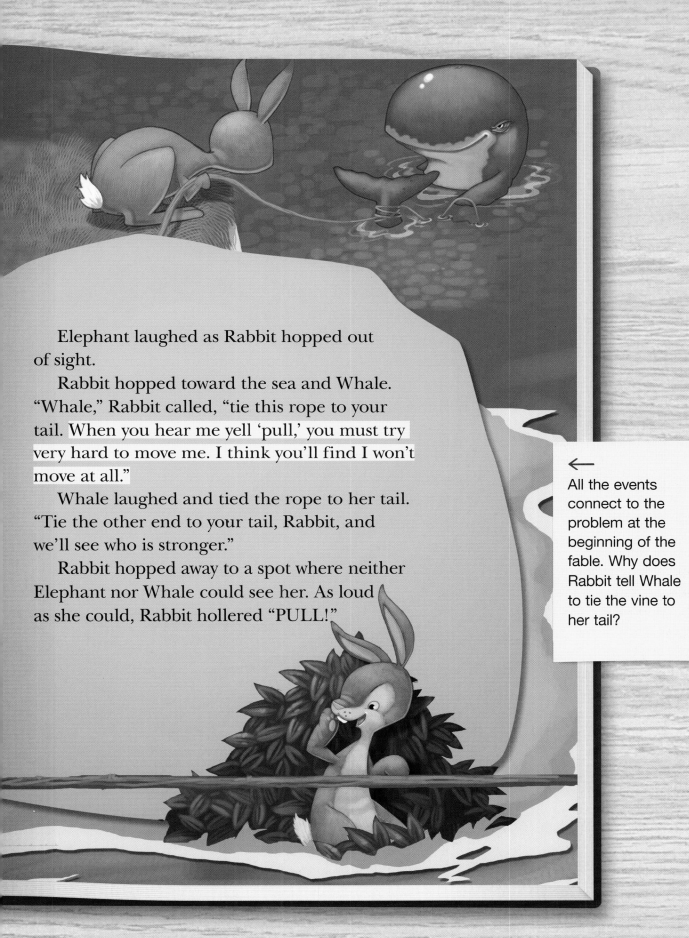

Elephant laughed as Rabbit hopped out of sight.

Rabbit hopped toward the sea and Whale. "Whale," Rabbit called, "tie this rope to your tail. When you hear me yell 'pull,' you must try very hard to move me. I think you'll find I won't move at all."

Whale laughed and tied the rope to her tail. "Tie the other end to your tail, Rabbit, and we'll see who is stronger."

Rabbit hopped away to a spot where neither Elephant nor Whale could see her. As loud as she could, Rabbit hollered "PULL!"

←

All the events connect to the problem at the beginning of the fable. Why does Rabbit tell Whale to tie the vine to her tail?

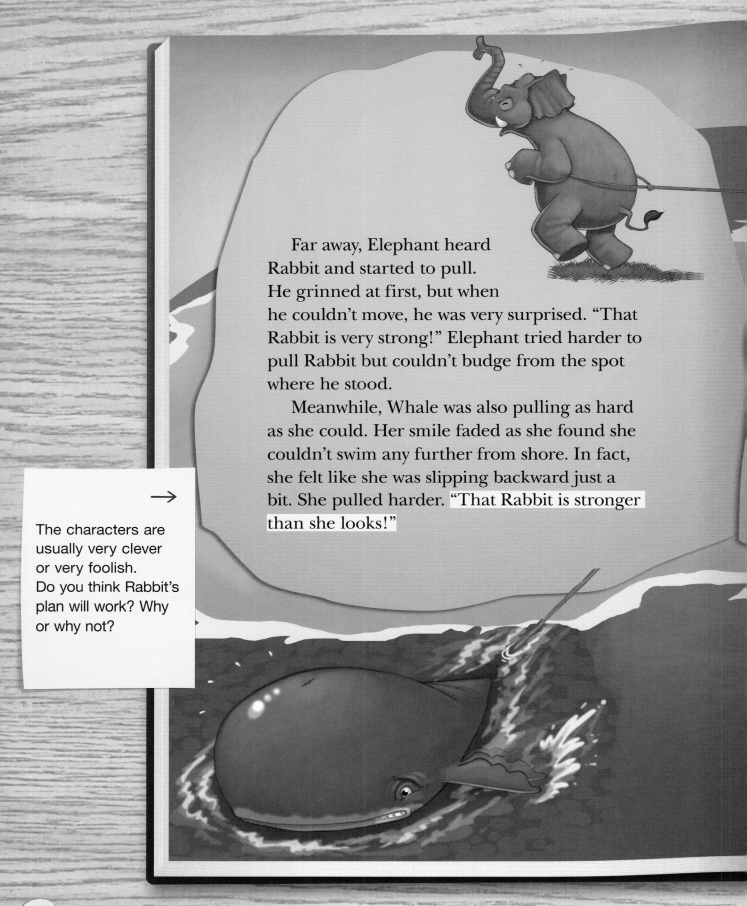

Far away, Elephant heard Rabbit and started to pull. He grinned at first, but when he couldn't move, he was very surprised. "That Rabbit is very strong!" Elephant tried harder to pull Rabbit but couldn't budge from the spot where he stood.

Meanwhile, Whale was also pulling as hard as she could. Her smile faded as she found she couldn't swim any further from shore. In fact, she felt like she was slipping backward just a bit. She pulled harder. "That Rabbit is stronger than she looks!"

→

The characters are usually very clever or very foolish. Do you think Rabbit's plan will work? Why or why not?

After a few more minutes of Whale and Elephant tugging at either end, the strong vine snapped. Elephant was pulling so hard on that vine, that when it snapped, he went crashing through the jungle and down a steep hill.

Of course, Whale was pulling just as hard. So when the vine snapped, she went spinning through the sea and smashed into a coral reef.

Rabbit quickly hopped away, not saying a word. From that day on, Elephant and Whale were always very polite to Rabbit and all other small animals.

Elephant and Whale never did figure out how such a tiny creature as Rabbit could have beaten the largest of the animals.

The characters are usually very clever or very foolish. Who do you think is clever in this fable? Who is foolish? Why do you think so?

Fables teach a lesson, which is often called the "moral." What lesson does this fable teach?

Moral: Strength is no match for intelligence.

Belling the Cat

An Aesop fable
Illustrated by Kyle Aleksander

Applying Strategies

Narrative: Identifying Characteristics of Fables

As you read, look for these characteristics of fables:

- The characters in fables are often animals.

- All the events connect to the problem at the beginning of the fable.

- The characters are usually very clever or very foolish.

- Fables teach a lesson, which is often called the "moral."

Mice and cats have been enemies forever. After all, it is a cat's job to chase, catch, and then eat mice.

In one farmhouse, the mice had been living for several years without any worries. The farmer kept the cat in the barn. There, the cat hunted the rats. Then one day, all the rats were gone. The farmer decided to bring the cat into the house.

The mice met to talk about the problem.

A young mouse complained, "Every time I poke my head out of a hole, the cat is there."

"Something has to be done," another mouse said.

"The cat chases us one at a time," pointed out an old mouse. "Maybe if we all chased the cat, we would scare it."

The grandmother mouse shook her head and said, "Well, we might frighten it at first. But after a while it would be back. And it would be angry!" She was a very wise mouse.

"You're right!" agreed the youngest mouse. "But if we could hear the cat coming, we could run away quickly."

"We could put a bell on the cat's collar. That way, we would always know where it was," suggested the first mouse.

Most of the mice thought belling the cat was a great idea. They knew they'd never have to worry about the cat again, if it was wearing a bell. All the younger mice hopped around happily.

But the grandmother mouse shook her head. "Which mouse will be brave enough to put a bell on the cat?" she asked.

Moral: Talk is easier than action.

Reflect on

Strategies: How do you know that this selection is a fable? Give examples from the story to support your thinking.

Critical Literacy: How might this fable be different if it were told from the cat's point of view?

THE CROW and the JUG

An Aesop fable retold by Michael Morpurgo
Illustrated by Anton Petrov

As you read, look for these characteristics of fables:

- The characters in fables are often animals.

- All the events connect to the problem at the beginning of the fable.

- The characters are usually very clever or very foolish.

- Fables teach a lesson, which is often called the "moral."

It was bone-dry in the countryside. There had been no rain for weeks on end now. For all the animals and birds, it had been a terrible time. To even find a drop of water to drink was almost impossible for them.

But the crow, being the cleverest of birds, always managed to fi keep himself alive.

One morning, as he flew over a cottage, he
saw a jug sta_____, of course,
knew that j_____s he flew
down, he c_____le. He
landed and _____look.

And sur_____e water at
the bottom. _____a little water
was a lot better than no water at all.

NEL

The crow stuck his head into the jug to drink; but his beak, long though it was, would not reach far enough down, no matter how hard he _____ he tried, but it was no _____

problem

However, the crow knew that one way or another, he had to drink that water. He stood there by the jug, wondering what he was going to do.

Then he saw pebbles lying on the ground nearby, and that gave him a brilliant idea.

One by one, he picked them up and dropped them into the jug. As each pebble fell to the bottom, the water in the jug rose a little higher, then higher and higher, until the crow had dropped so many pebbles in that the water was overflowing.

Now he could drink and drink his fill.

What a clever crow, he thought as he drank. *What a clever crow.*

Moral: Where there's a will, there's a way. But it helps if you use your brain.

Reflect on

Strategies: How do you know that this selection is a fable? Give examples from the story to support your thinking.

Your Learning: When might you use the trick the crow used in this fable?

Pig and Bear

A Czech fable retold by David Kherdian

Illustrated by Daron Parton

Applying Strategies

Narrative: Identifying Characteristics of Fables

As you read, look for these characteristics of fables:

- The characters in fables are often animals.

- All the events connect to the problem at the beginning of the fable.

- The characters are usually very clever or very foolish.

- Fables teach a lesson, which is often called the "moral."

There once was a pig and a bear who decided to go into business. They each rented a booth at the fair. Pig roasted a heap of potatoes. Bear fried up a batch of doughnuts.

They got to the fairgrounds early and set up their booths. It was a perfect day for selling steaming potatoes and fresh, warm doughnuts.

Bear had a nickel in his vest. Before any customers showed up, he went over to Pig's booth. "How much are you getting for one of those potatoes?" he asked.

"A nickel," Pig said.

Bear fished the nickel out of his pocket, laid it down on the counter, and picked up a steaming hot potato. He went back to his own booth and began eating his potato.

Business is good, Pig thought. Since no one was waiting in line, he walked over to Bear's booth and bought a strawberry-filled doughnut for a nickel.

Bear was pleased to have made a sale. Before another customer showed up, he thought he'd have something more to eat. He went over to Pig's booth and bought another potato.

The next thing Bear knew, Pig was over for another doughnut.

There wasn't any other business, until Bear bought another potato. Then Pig came over and bought a doughnut. Bear came back for another potato.

This happened several more times, back and forth, back and forth. Pig's and Bear's stomachs grew larger and larger.

HOT POTATOES

It wasn't long before all the potatoes and all the doughnuts were sold and eaten.

"I think it's time to count our money," Bear said to Pig.

When they did, they found that Bear had a nickel and Pig had nothing.

They couldn't believe their eyes.

"But we both sold out!" Pig cried. "Where's all our money?"

Bear looked down at his nickel and scratched his head. It wasn't until he had walked all the way back home that he realized it was the same nickel he had started with.

Moral: It's possible to be full of doughnuts and potatoes, and empty of common sense.

Reflect on

Strategies: How do you know that this story is a fable? Give examples from the story to explain your thinking.

Connections: What other stories do you know where characters do silly things that make you laugh?

Combining Sentences

Writers can make longer sentences by combining two or three short sentences. Using some longer sentences in your writing can give your work variety.

Short Sentences	Combined Sentence	
This fable is short. This fable is funny. This fable is surprising.	This fable is short, funny, and surprising.	You can combine short sentences that tell different things about the same subject.
Rabbit is clever. Crow is clever. Grandmother Mouse is clever.	Rabbit, Crow, and Grandmother Mouse are clever.	You can combine short sentences that tell the same thing about different subjects.
Bear started the day with a nickel. Bear bought potatoes. Bear sold doughnuts. Bear ended the day with a nickel.	Bear started the day with a nickel, bought potatoes, sold doughnuts, and ended the day with a nickel.	You can combine short sentences by using several action words in one longer sentence.

How to combine sentences:

☑ Look for two or more short sentences in a row.

☑ Read the sentences aloud. Think about what the sentences are saying.

☑ Try different ways of combining the sentences into one longer sentence.

Applying Strategies

Reading Like a Writer

As you read, identify places where the writer tells several things in one sentence.

The Owl and

An Inuit fable retold by David Kherdian
Illustrated by Aleks Sennwald

An owl saw a lemming feeding under a bush. "I must trick her into running so I can catch her," thought the owl. He flew down and said to the lemming, "Run! Two dog teams are coming!"

But the lemming knew what the owl was up to. She peered up at him from under the bush. Then she said, "You can have me to eat, Owl. I am quite plump and will make a good meal. But first, maybe you want to celebrate. I will be happy to sing while you dance."

the Lemming

The owl was overjoyed. He puffed himself up and began to dance to the lemming's tune. He looked up at the sky while he danced. Soon, he forgot all about the lemming. As the owl hopped from side to side, the lemming saw her chance. She dashed between the owl's legs and raced down her hole.

The owl called down to the lemming to come out, saying the dog teams had passed. But the wise lemming was safe now. So, she backed up in her hole and kicked dirt in the owl's face.

Moral: Do not be easily fooled.

Reflect on

Writer's Craft: Find a place where the writer told several things in one sentence. How did this add variety to the writing?

Your Learning: What qualities helped the lemming save herself from the owl?

Retelling

Retelling a story in your own words can help you understand and remember the story. After you've finished reading a story, retell it by thinking about

- the characters
- the problem
- the order of events
- the ending

Identify the problem at the beginning of the story. What problem is at the beginning of this fable?

Identify the characters in the story. Who is this fable about?

Fox and Crab Run a Race

A Chinese fable retold by Ling Ye
Illustrated by Bill Maguire

Fox was always boasting about how fast he was. "I'm the fastest animal around!" he told everyone.

To make it worse, Fox would say mean things to Crab about how slow she was. "Why do you crawl so slowly, Crab? You have twice as many legs as I do," Fox said with a cruel grin.

Crab became fed up. She thought of a way to stop Fox from boasting and teasing. "How would you like to race with me?" Crab asked Fox.

Fox looked at Crab in surprise. "Why would you want to race with me? I'll win. It wouldn't be fair."

Crab nodded. "Well, Fox, I don't think it is your legs that make you fast. Your tail is very big and it stands up straight in the air as you run. It catches the wind and acts like a sail. I think we should weight your tail down with something. Then we'll see if your legs really are faster than mine."

Identify events in the order they happen. What does Crab do because Fox makes fun of her?

→

Identify events in the order they happen. How does Fox react to Crab's suggestion?

↗

Identify events in the order they happen. What does Crab do?

Fox agreed. "You can tie a weight to my tail if you want, but I still don't think you'll win the race."

Crab smiled to herself as she crawled behind Fox. "Fox, I'm just going to tie something to your tail now. When I say 'Go,' you run."

"Right," said Fox.

Crab grabbed Fox's tail in her large claws.

"GO!" shouted Crab as loud as she could.

Fox jumped forward and ran as fast as he could. He didn't know Crab was holding onto his tail. So as fast as Fox ran, Crab was just as fast.

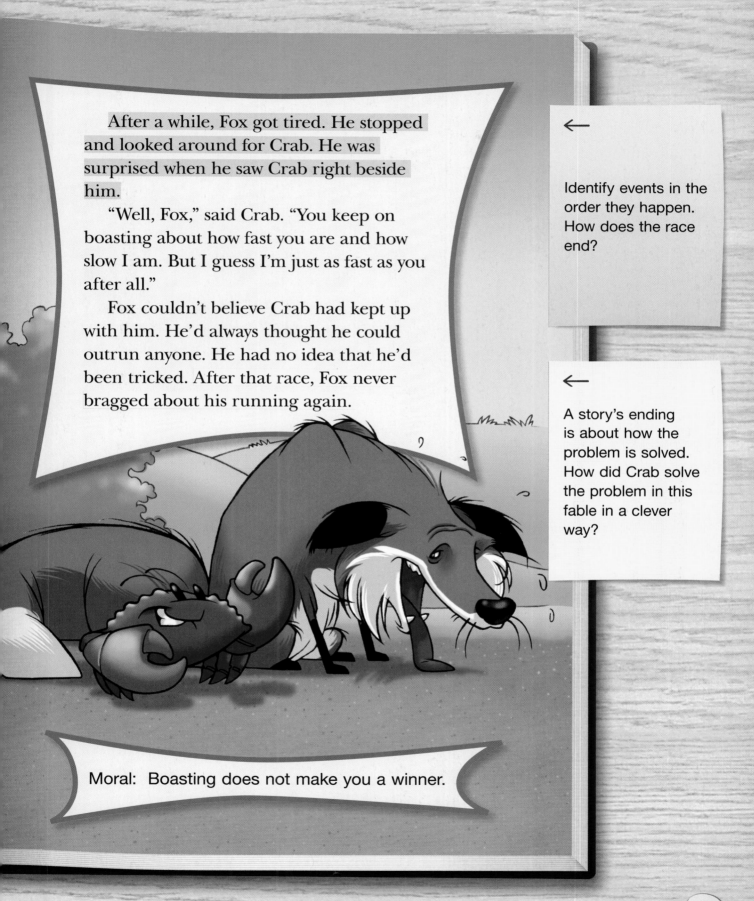

After a while, Fox got tired. He stopped and looked around for Crab. He was surprised when he saw Crab right beside him.

"Well, Fox," said Crab. "You keep on boasting about how fast you are and how slow I am. But I guess I'm just as fast as you after all."

Fox couldn't believe Crab had kept up with him. He'd always thought he could outrun anyone. He had no idea that he'd been tricked. After that race, Fox never bragged about his running again.

←

Identify events in the order they happen. How does the race end?

←

A story's ending is about how the problem is solved. How did Crab solve the problem in this fable in a clever way?

Moral: Boasting does not make you a winner.

The Fox and the Stork

An Aesop fable retold by Kendel Doyle
Illustrated by Jan-John Rivera

Fox liked to play tricks on his friends. One day Fox met his friend, Stork.

"Stork, would you like to have dinner with me tonight?" asked Fox.

"Of course! You are very kind," Stork answered.

"Excellent," Fox said. "I will make soup."

That night Stork went to Fox's house.

"Welcome," said Fox. "Come try my pond soup."

"It smells great," replied Stork. She was very hungry.

Fox went to the kitchen to serve the soup. He chuckled as he poured it into a flat dish.

"Here we are," said Fox. He placed the dish in front of Stork.

Stork sat down to eat. No matter how hard she tried, she couldn't eat the soup! The dish was too shallow for her long bill.

Stork didn't complain. She knew Fox had played a trick on her. As she was leaving she had an idea.

"Fox, I'd like to invite you to my house for lunch tomorrow."

Fox happily agreed.

Fox was very hungry when he got to Stork's house.

"Come try my soup," Stork said. She brought a tall jug out to Fox.

Fox started to eat, or tried to. But his tongue could not reach the soup! The jug was too narrow. Stork's long bill could reach far into the jug. She gobbled up all the soup.

Fox sighed, "I am starving! Stork, now I know, tricking you was not a smart plan."

Moral: A trickster can be beaten at his own game.

Reflect on

Strategies: How does retelling a fable help you understand what you have read?

Connections: How is this fable the same as or different from other fables you know?

The North Wind and the Sun

An Aesop fable
Illustrated by Noriko Senshu

Applying Strategies

Retelling

Retelling helps you to better understand the story. To help you retell this story, think about these things as you read:

- the characters
- the problem
- the order of events
- the ending

I AM STRONGER THAN YOU, SUN.

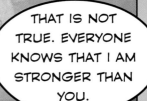

THAT IS NOT TRUE. EVERYONE KNOWS THAT I AM STRONGER THAN YOU.

SHOW ME THAT YOU ARE STRONGER THAN I AM. YOU KNOW VERY WELL THAT YOU ARE NOT.

DO YOU SEE THAT TRAVELLER? I CAN MAKE HIM TAKE OFF HIS COAT. YOU CANNOT.

WE WILL SEE ABOUT THAT. WHOEVER MAKES THE TRAVELLER TAKE OFF HIS COAT IS THE STRONGER ONE.

ALL RIGHT. YOU MAY GO FIRST.

WHEW! HOW THE NORTH WIND BLOWS. HOLD ON THERE, NORTH WIND; I WOULD RATHER WALK THAN FLY!

Moral: Often, gentleness works better than force.

Reflect on

Strategies: How does retelling a fable help you understand what you have read?

Connections: How is this fable the same as or different from other fables you know?

The Rabbits' Tale

A Chinese fable retold by Demi
Illustrated by David Hohn

Applying Strategies

Retelling

Retelling helps you to better understand the story. To help you retell this story, think about these things as you read:

- the characters
- the problem
- the order of events
- the ending

Once there was a family of rabbits who lived near a big fruit tree. One day, a large piece of fruit dropped off a branch, making a sound like thunder. The terrified rabbits ran away as fast as their legs could carry them. A fox asked, "Why are you running?"

"Because the sky is falling!" the rabbits replied, and so the fox followed them.

A few paces later, a monkey asked, "Why are you running?"

"The sky is falling!" the fox replied, and so the monkey ran, too.

Soon, a deer, a pig, a buffalo, a rhinoceros, an elephant, a bear, a leopard, and a tiger were all running from the falling sky.

They approached a lion. "Why are you all running?" he roared.

"Because the sky is falling!" they cried.

"How do you know?" the lion asked.

The tiger said the leopard had told him, the leopard said the bear had told him, the bear had been told by the elephant, who had been told by the rhinoceros, and so on. The rabbits squeaked, "Come, we'll show you where the sky fell."

They led the lion to the fruit tree and said, "The sky fell here!"

Just then, another big piece of fruit fell from the tree. The lion laughed and roared, "The sky has fallen again!"

Moral: If someone tells a falsehood, one hundred will repeat it as true.

Reflect on

Strategies: How does retelling a fable help you understand what you have read?

Connections: What other stories does this fable remind you of?

Using Tone and Volume

You can control your voice's tone and volume when you speak. Thinking about the tone and volume you use will make you a better speaker.

This student is practising a retelling of "Fox and Crab Run a Race." He wants to entertain his listeners. He tries different tones and volumes as he practises.

How to use tone and volume:

☑ Think about your purpose and your audience.

☑ Try out different tones and volumes. Listen to yourself.

☑ Choose the tone and volume that match the feeling you want to give your listeners.

Expressing Opinions

Expressing Personal Opinions about Illustrations

A story's illustrations can help you better understand the characters and events of the story. Readers don't always feel the same about an artist's illustrations. You can express your opinions about illustrations by describing what you like and don't like about them, and why.

These students are expressing their opinions about an illustration for the fable "The Tortoise and the Hare."

> THIS ILLUSTRATION IS FUN TO LOOK AT BECAUSE OF ALL THE DIFFERENT PATTERNS AND STITCHES IN THE FABRIC.

Give your opinion. What different opinions do these students give?

Give reasons for your opinion. Why does one student dislike the illustration? Why does another student like it?

Listen to the opinions of others. How does listening help these students have a good discussion?

> I DON'T LIKE IT BECAUSE IT LOOKS SLOPPY, LIKE A KID DID IT.

> BUT LOOK AT THE DETAILS— A SNAIL WITH THE RABBIT AND A BIRD ON THE TORTOISE. THE ARTIST IS REALLY THINKING ABOUT THE STORY. COOL!

Look at these illustrations from the fable "The Lion and the Mouse." What opinions do you have about the illustrations? What are the reasons for your opinions?

A Friend in Need

Written by Swapna Dutta

Illustrated by Jan-John Rivera

There once was a group of mice who lived in a forest near a river. A group of elephants lived in the same forest.

When the elephants rushed to the river to get a drink, they did not look where they were going. Many mice got crushed and their homes were destroyed. Something had to be done. But what could the little mice do? They were no match for the huge elephants.

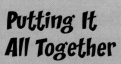

Finally, the leader of the mice
went to talk to the chief of the elephants.

The elephant chief was surprised. "What can
you possibly have to say to me?" she asked.

"Could you please ask the elephants to
take the path to the river? When they rush
through the trees, they trample the mice and
our homes."

The elephant said, "I'm sure they are not
aware of the damage they cause. They have no
reason to kill mice or destroy their homes. You
are far too tiny to be of any use! But I will ask
them to take the path to the river."

Then the elephant chief added, "I think you were brave to come to me, little mouse."

"Thank you, and if there is anything we can ever do to help you, we will do it," said the mouse.

This made the elephant burst out laughing!

"I can't imagine how a tiny creature like you can possibly help someone as huge as an elephant," said the chief, "but it was nice of you to offer."

The elephant chief kept her promise. She told the elephants to be careful and to go to the river without hurting the mice.

Then, one night, a band of elephant trappers snuck into the forest and trapped the elephants in huge nets. Even the elephant chief was caught.

The trappers had gone off to rest. They planned to take away the elephants the next morning.

"Can't anyone help us?" asked the trapped elephants.

"I can't think of anyone," said the chief in despair.

Luckily, the leader of the mice heard them. She was amazed to find all the elephants trapped.

"Don't worry, we'll have you free in no time," she said.

"Can you really do it?" asked the elephant chief.

"Of course," said the mouse. "I'll go and get the others."

The leader soon returned with the entire troop of mice. They attacked the nets with their sharp teeth. They worked all night. By morning, they had freed all the elephants from the traps.

"I thank you with all my heart," said the leader of the elephants gratefully. "I did not think that someone so small could help us out of such a serious situation. But now I know that size does not matter. You are true friends."

Moral: Little friends may prove to be great friends.

Reflect on

Strategies: How does thinking about the characteristics of fables help you plan a retelling of this fable?

Your Learning: How do fables help people think about themselves and others?

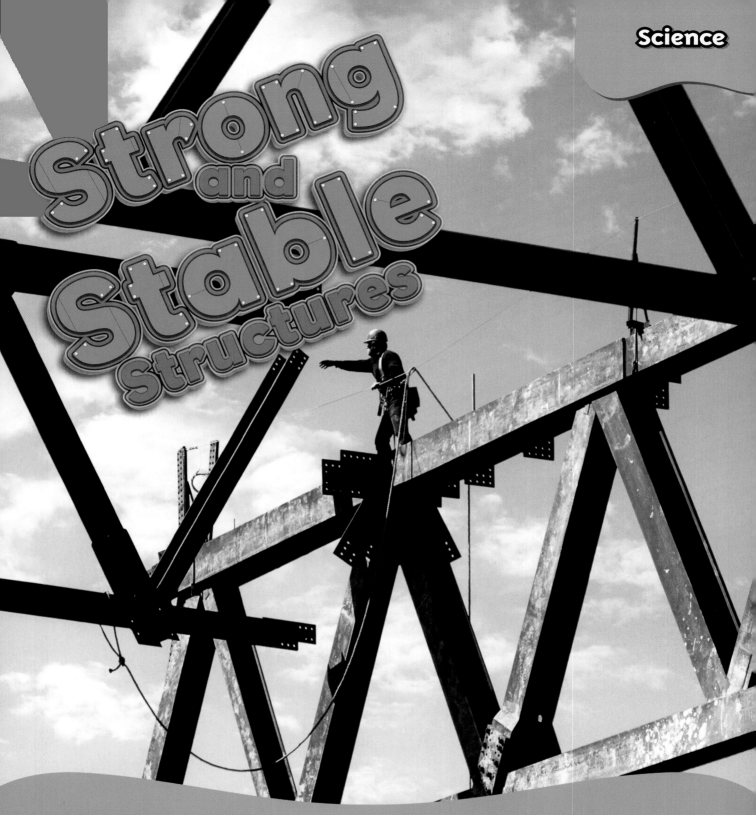

Strong and Stable Structures

In this unit, you will

- monitor comprehension

- read labelled visuals

- use labelled visuals when speaking

- vary sentence types

- learn about structures

- explain why different audiences respond differently to media texts

Structures in Our World

roller coaster

office building

igloo

All structures are useful. What is each of these structures used for?

bird nest

rocking chair

tent

Monitoring Comprehension

Monitoring comprehension means checking to make sure you understand what you are reading. When you get stuck, you can use fix-up strategies to help you.

→

Make sure you understand new words and ideas. What are some examples of structures?

What Do You Know about Structures?

by Janice Parker

What Is a Structure?

Look up. Is there a ceiling over your head? If there is, it is probably held up by walls that stand on a floor. You are inside a building of some kind. A building is a type of structure. Houses, bridges, tunnels, stores, and schools are all structures. Most structures are built to be strong and to keep out the forces of nature, such as wind, snow, and rain.

◄ Some houses are made from materials found in nature.

Structures come in many shapes and sizes. Some structures provide shelter and safety. Others, like bikes and planes, help us get from place to place.

Structures are made from many different materials. Some are made of clay, straw, or other materials found in nature. Others are built with materials people make, such as steel, glass, or concrete.

People have been building structures for thousands of years. Some animals build structures, too. A bird nest is one example.

Stop to ask yourself, "Does this make sense?" Why are structures useful?

▲ Not all structures are buildings. Buses, cars, and trucks are also structures.

◄ Concrete and bricks are used to build strong structures where people live and work.

Building Materials

Structures can be made from many types of materials. Some materials are better than others for building certain kinds of structures. For example, glass is the best material for building an aquarium, which is a place where fish live.

→

Read ahead to get information about new words or ideas. What types of materials are used for building structures?

→

→

Use photos, illustrations, and charts to help you understand new words and ideas. What information will you find in this chart?

Types of Building Materials

Stone

- found in nature
- strong and long lasting
- can be used whole or cut into blocks

Clay

- a type of soil
- soft and sticky when wet, hard when dry
- can be made into bricks

Wood

- comes from trees
- easy to use
- can be held together with nails

Concrete

- like stone, but made by people
- strong when dry
- can be poured into any shape when wet

Glass

- made from melted sand
- light shines through it
- can be made in many colours

Steel

- made from metals
- very strong
- can be melted and moulded into shapes

Use photos, illustrations, and charts to help you understand new words and ideas. How is concrete different from wood? How is concrete like steel?

Animal Homes

by Angela Wilkes

Applying Strategies

Monitoring Comprehension

As you read, check your understanding. If you get stuck:

- Make sure you understand new words and ideas.

- Stop to ask yourself, "Does this make sense?"

- Read ahead to get information about new words or ideas.

- Use photos, illustrations, and charts to help you understand new words and ideas.

Animals need homes, just like people do. Homes keep animals warm in the winter. They are a safe place to have babies. Some animals make structures to live in.

A Snowy Home

Polar bears live in cold, snowy places. A mother polar bear makes a home called a *den*. She digs her den in snow. In the winter, she has her babies in the den.

A Paper Home

A wasp nest is a structure made of paper. Wasps make paper by chewing up wood. Baby wasps grow up inside the nest.

A Nest for Babies

Birds make nests for their eggs. A nest is warm and away from danger. Most birds make nests in trees.

Make a Nest

What You Need

- paintbrush and glue
- plastic bowl
- dried grass
- moss
- feathers and leaves
- candy wrappers

What You Do

1. Use the paintbrush to spread glue on the outside of the bowl. Stick small handfuls of grass onto the bowl.

2. Spread glue on the inside of the bowl. Stick grass and moss inside the bowl.

3. Put some small feathers and leaves inside the nest. Add some candy wrappers for colour.

Reflect on

Strategies: How did looking at photos help you check your understanding about what you were reading?

Connections: What animal homes have you seen? What were they made of?

DOME HOME

by Etta Kaner

soldier crab

Applying Strategies

Monitoring Comprehension

As you read, check your understanding. If you get stuck,

- Make sure you understand new words and ideas.

- Stop to ask yourself, "Does this make sense?"

- Read ahead to get information about new words or ideas.

- Use photos, illustrations, and charts to help you understand new words and ideas.

GETTING INTO SHAPE

Animal homes come in all kinds of shapes. Each animal builds a home that is shaped for its needs.

Soldier crabs build sand homes shaped like domes. A soldier crab works hard to build its home.

Soldier crabs often move in a large group. They look like an army of marching soldiers.

As Strong As An Egg

Hold the ends of an egg between the palms of your hands. Now press as hard as you can. It's impossible to break it, right? That's because each end of the egg is a dome, which is a very strong shape. No wonder a soldier crab builds its shelter in the shape of a dome.

The soldier crab stays in its shelter while the tide is in. The shelter protects it from drowning. Then the crab digs its way out of the shelter when the tide goes out.

The dome shape at each end of an egg makes it hard to break.

Building a Dome Home

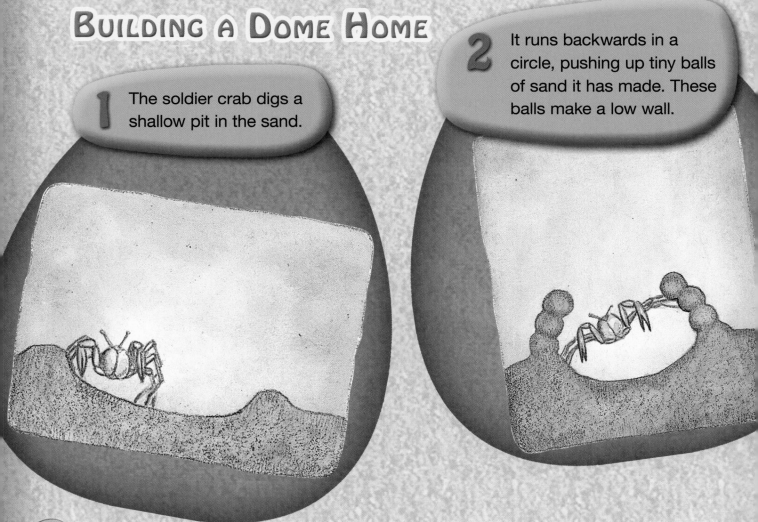

1 The soldier crab digs a shallow pit in the sand.

2 It runs backwards in a circle, pushing up tiny balls of sand it has made. These balls make a low wall.

3 The crab continues to push up balls of sand. The wall gets higher and higher, and finally curves in.

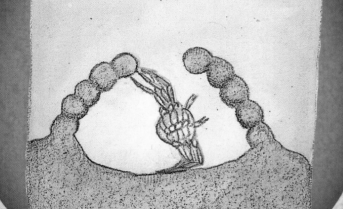

4 It fills in the hole at the top with a tiny ball of sand.

5 Finally, it makes the top thicker by pushing up more sand from the bottom.

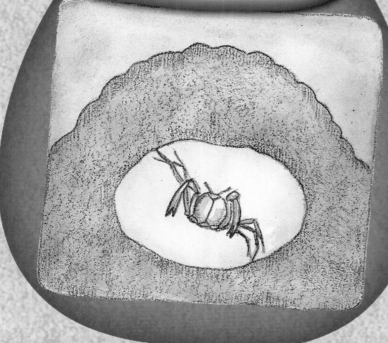

Reflect on

Strategies: How did the visuals help you understand new ideas in the article?

Your Learning: What did you learn about the shape of a dome?

The Wonder of Beavers

by Amy Bauman and Patricia Corrigan

If you hike through the woods near the end of the day, you might be lucky enough to spot a very busy and hard-working creature. If you see a large, dark animal swimming in the water, it could be a beaver!

Beavers have wide flat tails. They use their tails to help them build.

Beavers are animals that live along rivers, lakes, and ponds in North America and Europe. They like both water and land. Beavers are best known for the dams they build in their watery habitats.

Beavers are some of nature's best builders. They build dams in rivers, marshes, and lakes. Some dams are as long as two football fields!

A beaver built this dam from branches and mud. A dam is a structure that stops water from flowing.

Beavers build dams out of branches, stones, and mud. First, they cut down trees with their front teeth. Then they bite off the branches and drag them into the water.

Beavers usually work alone. Sometimes, beaver families, called *colonies*, will work together on big projects.

A beaver's front teeth are long, orange, and sharp!

Often, a beaver colony lives together in a home called a *lodge*. The lodge is made of sticks and mud. Each lodge has one big room.

Beavers live in structures called lodges. Most lodges are about 5 m wide and 2 m high.

Inside the lodge, beavers will build the floor above the water to keep it dry. They cover the floor with soft grasses. The colony sleeps here.

Beavers go in and out of the lodge through tunnels. They also escape from enemies through these tunnels.

Here you can see the inside of a beaver lodge.

The beaver will use this branch to build a dam or a lodge.

Some people think beavers harm the environment because they cut down too many trees. Other people believe beavers are helpful to the environment. Beaver dams can become homes for other animals. Dams can also stop a stream from drying up, or land from eroding.

The beaver is a clever and useful creature. You would be lucky to spot a busy beaver someday!

Reflect on

Strategies: What strategies did you use when you got stuck?

Critical Literacy: How might someone who thinks beavers harm the environment write about beavers? What title might they use?

Dream House

Explaining Why Different Audiences Respond Differently to Media Texts

What is your dream house? Different people would answer this question in different ways.

Thinking about connections can help you understand different feelings about the same house. What connections can you make to this house? What connections might your grandparents make?

Making inferences can help you understand different feelings about the same house. What kinds of books or movies or games might the owners of this house enjoy?

Visualizing can help you understand different feelings about the same house. Who can you visualize answering the door in this house? Who might look out of place answering the front door?

Who do you think would look at this house and say,
"My dream house!" Who might not feel at home here?

Varying Sentence Types

Imagine a world with only one kind of fruit. That would be boring! We all like variety. Readers like variety, too, and you can keep them interested if you learn how to vary the types of sentences you use when you write.

Here are some different types of sentences you can use in your writing:

→ This is a question.

Have you ever seen the CN Tower?

This is a simple sentence. ←

The CN Tower is tall and strong.

Think of all the problems people solved to build the tower.

← This is a command. It tells the reader to do something.

→ This is an exclamatory sentence. It shows strong emotion.

The CN Tower is an amazing structure!

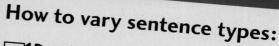

How to vary sentence types:

☑ Read your writing out loud.

☑ Identify the different sentence types you used.

☑ Try different sentence types to add variety.

Applying Strategies

Reading Like a Writer

As you read, identify different sentence types. Think about how the variety in sentence types helps make the writing interesting.

MAIL A POSTCARD!

COME VISIT A TEEPEE

Dear Jenny,

We went to an Aboriginal powwow. The singing and dancing were great! Then we saw teepees, and they are really interesting. Did you know teepees were made of animal skins wrapped around poles?

I learned that teepees are waterproof. In winter they are warm, and in summer they stay cool. I wish we could use a teepee when we go camping.

Write me soon!

Your friend,
Kayla

TO:

Jenny Tremain

7 Wilkes Crescent

Calgary, AB T2N 3T4

Hi Tom,

Today we stopped in Ottawa to see the National Gallery of Canada. It's amazing! The big tower is made of glass. Would you want to be the person who has to clean it?

All that glass is really heavy, so there is a steel frame to hold it up. The view from inside the tower is great. You can see the Parliament Buildings.

Come to Ottawa sometime. It's a fun city!

See you soon,
Rajiv

TO:

Tom Campbell
46 Redmond Road
Halifax, NS B3N 2K1

National Gallery of Canada

Reflect on

Writer's Craft: Find examples of three different types of sentences. Explain how these make the writing interesting.

Connections: Write an exclamatory sentence about a place you've visited.

Text Features: Labelled Visuals

Illustrations and photos, or visuals, help readers understand what they are reading. Labels point out important parts in visuals.

→

Labelled visuals help readers understand what they are reading. What does the labelled photo on this page help you understand?

The Pyramids of Egypt

by Boris Brodsky

Building Big

It's not easy to build a big structure that is strong and stable enough to last for thousands of years. But the ancient Egyptians did it. They built pyramids. The most amazing pyramid of all is called The Great Pyramid.

Why have some Egyptian pyramids lasted so long?

140 m tall

2 million blocks in the pyramid

A Strong Shape

Some shapes help a structure last a long time. A pyramid starts out big at the bottom and gets smaller as it goes up. This helps to make it strong and stable.

Building with Stone

The Egyptians used stone to build the pyramids. Stone is a very strong building material. It can support the weight of a heavy building. And it lasts a very long time.

To make stone blocks the right size, workers hammered pieces of wood into the stone. Then they poured on water. The wood got bigger as it soaked up the water. That made the stone split.

Labelled visuals help readers understand what they are reading. What does the visual on this page help you understand?

Labels point out important parts in visuals. What should you notice in this labelled illustration?

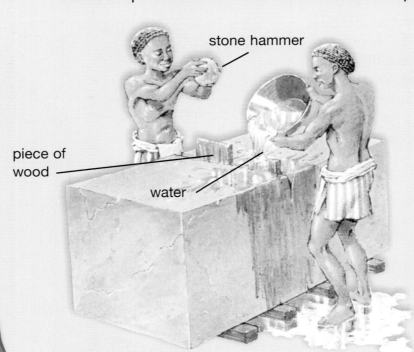

stone hammer

piece of wood

water

Shaping the Blocks

The workers had to carefully smooth and shape the blocks by hand. Each block had to fit exactly in place. That helps to keep the pyramid strong and stable.

Moving the Blocks

The stone blocks used to build the pyramids are big—and very heavy! How did ancient Egyptians move these blocks? Most people believe they used ramps made of dirt. It took many workers to drag the blocks up the ramp. Logs placed under the blocks made them easier to move.

workers moving blocks into place

ramp

stone block

Labelled visuals help readers understand what they are reading. What does this visual help you understand?

←

Labels point out important parts in visuals. What should you notice in this labelled illustration?

A Pyramid That Didn't Last

Some pyramids were not as strong and stable as others. The pyramid you see here is much smaller than the Great Pyramid, and it is not as old. Now it is falling apart. The workers did not make it as strong and stable as the Great Pyramid.

The pyramid of Sahure, in Egypt, has crumbled over time.

A Modern Pyramid

In France, there is a modern pyramid built of steel and glass. These are strong building materials, so this pyramid will last a long time. Will it last for thousands of years, like the pyramids in Egypt? It's hard to say. What do you think?

This modern glass pyramid is the entrance to the Louvre Museum in Paris, France.

Tunnels
Underground

by Craig Shackleton

Applying Strategies

Text Features: Labelled Visuals

As you read, use what you know about labelled visuals:

- Labelled visuals help readers understand what they are reading.

- Labels point out important parts in visuals.

Tunnels Big and Small

A tunnel is a long hole under the ground. Many animals dig tunnels to live in. Have you ever seen an anthill? The ants live in tiny tunnels they have dug under the hill.

Anthill

entrance

underground tunnel

People also dig tunnels. We build big tunnels for cars, trucks, and trains to go through. Some tunnels go right through mountains! These tunnels can take a long time to build.

machine that digs tunnels

dirt and rock

moving belt

Building a Tunnel

There are special machines that dig tunnels. These machines cut through dirt and rock. A moving belt carries the dirt and rock that have been cut away.

The dirt and rock are dumped into train cars. Then the train drives over to an elevator.

elevator

tunnel wall

train car

The elevator lifts the dirt and rock out of the tunnel so trucks can carry it away.

Workers build strong walls inside the tunnel. These walls keep the tunnel from caving in.

Sometimes people build tunnels under water. These tunnels have to be very strong so they are safe. No one wants a tunnel to cave in!

Reflect on

Strategies: How did labelled visuals help you understand what you were reading?

Connections: Why is it dangerous for children to dig snow tunnels?

Getting to

by Todd Mercer

Amanda, Jared, and their mom had a problem. They were hiking along a nature trail when they saw that a stream flowed right across their path.

The three hikers sat down in a shady spot. "What do we do now?" asked Jared. "I don't want to finish our hike with soaking wet feet."

Suddenly Amanda cried out, "Look!" and she pointed to some bushes. "I think I see a board over there."

Mom, Amanda, and Jared went over to investigate. They found a long board.

"This might be the answer to our problem," said Jared.

the Other Side

Mom and Jared dragged the board to the stream. Then they placed the board across the stream to make a bridge.

"Do you think this bridge is strong enough to hold us up?" asked Amanda.

"I'm the heaviest person," said Mom. "I'll test it." She started to walk slowly across the bridge.

rocks supporting each end of bridge

board sagging from Mom's weight

Then Jared called out, "Come back, Mom! The board is starting to sag. When you get to the middle, the board will sag right down into the water."

"It might even break!" said Amanda.

Mom carefully came back. "So what do we do now?" she asked.

"We need something to support the bridge in the middle," said Amanda. "That's where it will sag the most."

"There's a rock in the middle of the stream just over there," said Jared. "Let's move the board so the rock is underneath it. The rock will support the bridge so it won't sag too much."

"It's worth a try," said Mom.

rocks supporting each end of the bridge

rock supporting the middle of the bridge

Mom and Amanda moved the board so that it rested on the rock in the stream. Mom tested the bridge. It was strong enough to hold her up. Everyone crossed the stream without getting wet.

"Good work, kids," said Mom. "Thanks to you two, we all have dry feet!"

Reflect on

Strategies: How did labelled visuals help you understand what you were reading?

Your Learning: How did knowing about bridges help the family solve a problem? When might your knowledge of bridges help you?

Using Labelled Visuals

It's exciting to teach other people how to do something you had fun doing. Labelled visuals can help you explain ideas to listeners.

Vicky used labelled photos to help her give a presentation to her class. She explained how she made a pencil holder.

TRACE A CIRCLE ON THE CARDBOARD AND CUT IT OUT. GLUE THE CIRCLE OVER ONE END OF THE TOILET PAPER ROLL. LET IT DRY.

circle

USE THE PAINTBRUSH TO SPREAD GLUE OVER THE OUTSIDE OF THE ROLL. PUT THE CRAFT STICKS NEXT TO EACH OTHER TO COVER THE ROLL.

sticks glued on tube

PUT RUBBER BANDS AROUND THE STICKS UNTIL THE GLUE IS DRY.

rubber bands

TAKE OFF THE RUBBER BANDS AND DECORATE THE PENCIL HOLDER WITH STICKERS.

stickers

How to use labelled visuals:

☑ **Think about what you want to tell your listeners.**

☑ **Take photos or draw pictures.**

☑ **Use labels to show what is important in each visual.**

Skyscrapers

by Elaine Landau

Superman leaped over them. Kids love to ride in elevators up to the top of them. Have you ever been in a *very* tall building that rises far above the rest? If you have, it was probably a skyscraper.

Giants in the Sky

Skyscrapers seem to touch the sky. Most are at least 35 floors high, and some have more than 100 floors. Many skyscrapers are more than just tall. Inside, you may find hotels, restaurants, stores, and hundreds of offices. A skyscraper is like a small world!

Putting It All Together

As you read, remember to use the strategies you've learned in this unit:

- Monitor your comprehension.

- Use labelled visuals to help you understand what you are reading.

- Identify different sentence types.

Parts of a Skyscraper

A skyscraper has two main parts. One is the foundation. You do not see that part because it lies beneath the ground. The foundation is made of steel or sometimes concrete. It stands on a layer of solid rock or soil. The foundation helps to hold up the rest of the building. A parking garage is often inside the foundation.

The other part of a skyscraper is called the *superstructure*. That is the part of the building that is above the ground.

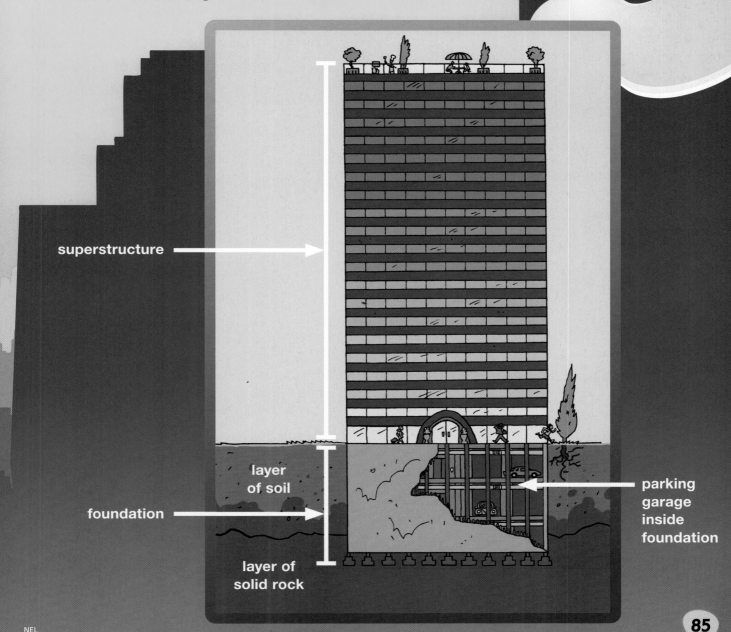

superstructure

foundation

layer of soil

layer of solid rock

parking garage inside foundation

A Skyscraper's Skeleton

In a building with one or two floors, the walls hold up the building. A skyscraper needs a frame to hold it up. This frame is made of steel, or of concrete with steel inside.

In some ways, a skyscraper's frame is like a human skeleton. Your skeleton is made up of bones. These bones make a frame to hold up your body. A frame made of steel or steel and concrete holds up a skyscraper. The building's walls are attached to the outside of the frame. You cannot see the frame when the building is finished. Like your skeleton, the frame is in there, doing its job.

A strong steel frame will hold up this skyscraper.

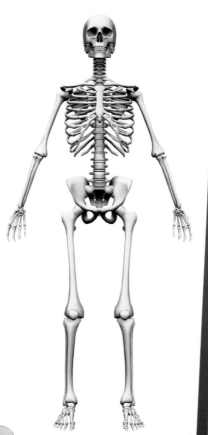

The bones of your skeleton make a frame that holds up your body.

Planning a Skyscraper

Lots of planning goes into building a skyscraper. Many people work on designing the building. They decide on the skyscraper's shape and the materials that will be used to build it. People work hard to make the skyscraper strong enough to stand up to things like storms and earthquakes.

Strong winds can be a problem, too. A skyscraper must not sway back and forth too much in the wind. Too much swaying could cause problems for the elevators. It could also crack the glass on the outside of the building.

A lot of time and work goes into designing and building skyscrapers, but the rewards are sky-high!

People make diagrams called *blueprints* to plan a skyscraper.

Tall and Taller

All skyscrapers are tall, but some are taller than others. On this page, you can see some of the tallest skyscrapers in the world.

New skyscrapers are being built all the time. People are always trying to break the record for the world's tallest skyscraper.

Name: Taipei 101
Location: Taiwan
Height: 509 m
Number of floors: 101

Name: Petronas Twin Towers
Location: Malaysia
Height: 452 m
Number of floors: 88

Reflect on

Strategies: What strategies did you use when you were reading this article? Find a place where you used a strategy to help you.

Your Learning: Find three facts about skyscrapers that you would like to remember.

Soils in the Environment

In this unit, you will

- identify characteristics of question-and-answer text pattern

- learn to give an oral report

- synthesize information

- use text features in published reports

- describe the main elements of seed packages

- learn about soils

The Soil Is Alive!

Look at this picture. Describe five living things that you see in the soil.

Identifying Characteristics of Question-and-Answer Text Pattern

Question-and-answer text pattern is a way of organizing information. Each question introduces what the section will be about. Answers give information about the topic.

→

Each question introduces what the section will be about. What is the topic of this section?

ASK THE SOIL SCIENTIST

by Diane Robitaille

What is soil?

You might know it as dirt or earth. *Soil* is just another word to describe what's under your feet when you're outside. Our Earth is covered in a thin layer of soil.

Why is soil important?

All living things need soil. Most plants grow in soil. Many animals eat those plants. Other animals eat the animals that eat those plants. Without soil, you might never again have a strawberry milkshake or a hamburger with fries.

Grass grows in soil.   A cow eats the grass.   Some people drink milkshakes and eat hamburgers. Milk and beef come from a cow.

What is soil made of?

Here is a simple recipe for soil. Take some dead plants and some dead animals, mix in tiny bits of rock, and then add water and air. You'll need to add in some bacteria, too. Bacteria are living things that are so small we can't see them without a special tool called *a microscope*.

Then you'll need to add time to the mixture. Making soil can take thousands of years. Different types of weather, such as rain, sun, and cold, also help break up rocks and create soil.

Answers give information about the topic. What is soil made of?

→

Each question introduces what the section will be about. What will you learn in this section?

What are the different layers of soil?

The top layer of soil right under your feet is called *topsoil*. It is dark because it usually has lots of rotting plants and animals in it. Plant roots grow here.

The next layer down is the *subsoil*. It is usually light brown because it has fewer rotting plants and animals than the topsoil. It also contains more rocks.

Deeper down is the *parent material*. This layer may be grey or yellowish-brown because it is made up of clay, sand, and larger rocks.

You won't be able to dig down into the next layer. It's solid rock!

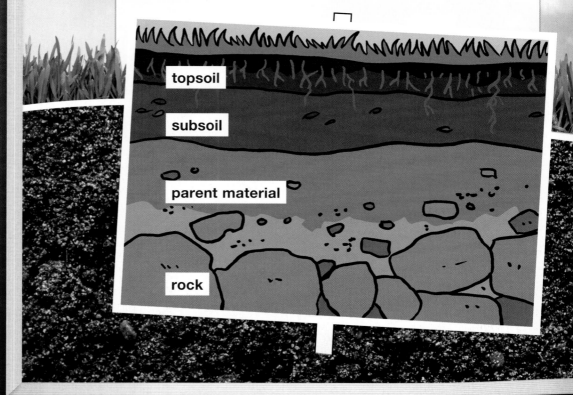

topsoil

subsoil

parent material

rock

Is there just one type of soil?

Definitely not! Soil can come in many colours and textures. Soil can be brown, red, black, or grey. Soil can be dry and sandy. Soil can be wet and hard. Different soils are good for growing different types of plants. Cactus plants grow really well in dry, sandy soil. Cranberry plants grow best in swamps that have a rich, wet soil.

Answers give information about the topic. What do you find out about the types of soil in this answer?

dry, sandy soil

red clay soil

rich black topsoil

Surprising Soil

by Ethan Elliot

How many living things are there in soil?

Millions! Thousands of spiders, worms, and insects can live in just one small square of soil. Insects like ants and beetles are easy to see. A water bear can be seen only with a microscope. Foxes and rabbits live in soil, too. They live in holes in the ground or in the sides of hills. Tiny plants called *algae* grow inside soil. They look like green pieces of string.

A mole moves through the soil using its claws. Its strong arms easily push soil out of its way.

Can you eat off plates made from soil?

Clay is part of soil. When you mix clay with water, you can shape it into plates, pots, and cups. Pottery is then baked in an oven or by the sun until it hardens. Clay pottery is very strong and lasts a long time.

People have found clay pots that are over 10 000 years old.

Is mud good for your skin?

Yes. Mud contains vitamins and minerals. In some parts of the world, people use mud to treat burns and insect bites. Mud baths can help tired muscles feel better.

Are windows made from soil?

Windows are made from glass. Glass is made from a type of sand called *silica*. And you guessed it! Sand is a part of soil. So, yes, windows are made from soil. To make glass, the sand is heated until it melts. Then it is cooled slowly.

White sand makes the clearest glass.

Can you eat soil?

Never eat soil. Besides tasting yucky, it could make you very sick. Why? Gardeners sometimes add animal manure to soil. Harmful chemicals and bacteria are also in soil.

Reflect on

Strategies: How can previewing questions help you predict what you will learn in an article?

Connections: What did you already know about soil before reading this text? What did you learn?

Animals Love MUD

Mud dauber wasps build their mud nests on the outside of houses, barns, and sheds.

Animals all over the world use mud to help them live.

How do wasps use mud?

Some wasps use balls of mud to build long fingerlike tubes where they store dead spiders. The wasps lay eggs on the spiders. When the eggs hatch, the baby wasps eat the spiders. After three weeks, the baby wasps spin cocoons and spend the winter in their mud homes.

Why do flamingos make mud nests?

Flamingos may look like they're making mud pies with their curved beaks, but they're not. They are making huge mud nests. The large nests protect the flamingos' eggs and babies from the hot ground and from rising water that could flood the nests.

Flamingos use their beaks to pile mud on the shores of lakes and rivers.

Where do cliff swallows build their mud nests?

Cliff swallows use mud to build cup-shaped nests on high cliffs, on rock walls, and even under bridges. Their small nests are lined with feathers and grasses. The nest is a cozy home for the eggs and young chicks.

How do reptiles use mud?

Reptiles such as alligators and crocodiles use mud to build nests. An alligator piles up mud and plants, and then lays eggs in the middle of the pile. The Nile crocodile digs a hole in the mud and lays eggs in it. The crocodile then covers up the hole with mud.

This alligator is protecting its eggs.

Rhinos like this one cover their horns in mud first, and then lie down and roll from side to side.

Why do some animals wear mud?

Mud keeps the animals' skin cool. Rhinoceroses, warthogs, and elephants cover themselves in mud from head to tail. The mud also dries into a hard, crusty coat that stops mosquitoes from biting the animal.

Why do some birds shower with dirt?

Pheasants, wrens, and house sparrows follow a water bath with a shower of dirt. Their feathers would become matted if they didn't. That's because these birds spread oil from their bodies over their feathers to waterproof them. The dirt soaks up the extra oil, keeping their feathers in great shape.

In the wild, moose will eat or lick mud.

Why do some animals eat mud?

Mud contains nutrients and minerals that some animals need. Moose eat or lick mud. One type of parrot eats mud because the mud soaks up the poison from the seeds and fruit the parrot has eaten.

Reflect on

Strategies: How can knowing about question-and-answer text pattern help you find information you are looking for?

Your Learning: What did you learn about animals and mud that you would share with a friend?

Organizing an Oral Report

When you give an oral report, your listeners want to learn from you. Make your information easy to understand by organizing it clearly in chunks. These students used question-and-answer text pattern to organize their oral report.

How to organize an oral report using questions and answers:

- ✔ Look for chunks of information that fit together.
- ✔ Write a question for each chunk of information.
- ✔ Answer each question for your listeners.

Synthesizing

Synthesizing means using information from different places to build a new understanding of a topic. Think about what you already know. Gather information from text, visuals, and captions. When you fit this information together, you are synthesizing.

Think about what you already know. This article is about earthworms. What do you know about earthworms?

↙

WIGGLY WORMS

by Aaron Meleski

Hi, I'm an earthworm. You've probably seen me and my friends in your garden, on your grass, or even on the sidewalk after a rainy day. Please don't step on me. Earthworms do great things for the soil.

Earthworms turn rotting leaves and animals into food for plants.

Gather information from the text. Why did the earthworm spend the day deep under the vegetable garden?

→

It was really sunny out today, so I stayed deep under the vegetable garden. I don't like the sun. It dries up my skin. I said "hi" to a few friends and then got to work slithering through the soil, mixing the soil layers together.

I was really hungry today. I munched on soil, dead leaves, and insects. I gobbled all that tasty food up with my mouth. From there, the food slid into my crop, and then down to my gizzard. I don't have any teeth to chew my food with. I have muscles that help me digest my food.

tail

setae

An earthworm's digestive system has many parts.

mouth

crop

gizzard

intestine

← Gather information from visuals. What does the text tell you about how earthworms eat? What does the diagram show you?

After I finished eating, little pellets called *castings* came out of my tail. Castings make great food for plants because they are packed with nutrients and minerals.

Castings help soak up water that the soil needs.

Gather information from captions. How do earthworm castings help grow healthy plants?

←

I had a fright near the end of the day. A little girl dug me up with her shovel! I wriggled off the shovel and into the dirt before she saw me. I took some bits of dead grass and leaves as I went.

Worms like to eat dead leaves with pointed ends.

Fit information together to build a new understanding. Why do you see earthworms on rainy days and not sunny days?

It's not safe for worms to be out of the soil for too long. We need the moist soil to help us breathe. The only time we come out is at nighttime and after it rains.

When it rains, worms' burrows fill up with water. If they don't come above the ground, they will drown.

One time a worm friend of mine had a tiny piece of his tail cut off. He was okay. He grew another tail. That's because our bodies are made out of segments. We worms can keep living if we have enough segments left.

An earthworm can grow a new tail or head if it is cut close to the first and last segments.

Phew! It's a lot of work twisting, tunnelling, and eating through the soil. Did you know I eat my weight in soil every day? It's true. The hard work is worth it. I help the soil grow healthy flowers, and vegetables.

There may be as many as 30 hard-working worms in a bucket of good garden soil.

← Gather information from text, visuals, and captions. What happens to an earthworm if its tail gets cut off?

Fit information together to build a new understanding. Why do gardeners like to see earthworms?

Mud Houses

by Carmen Petrovic

Applying Strategies

Synthesizing

As you read, remember to use the strategy of synthesizing:

- Think about what you already know.
- Gather information from text, visuals, and captions.
- Fit information together to build a new understanding.

Some people live in mud houses. Mud is easy to find and doesn't cost anything. Mud houses stay cool on hot days and stay warm on cold days. These houses last for a very long time. Some mud houses are over 10 000 years old.

Mud houses can crack. People can repair them by spreading on new mud.

Where did people get the idea to build mud houses? From animals, such as termites and beavers!

How do you build a mud house? First you mix mud with straw and grass. Next, you spread this wet mud over a twig frame. Then, the sun bakes the mud until it is hard.

Termites' nests are under the soil. Termites build mud towers on top of their nests to protect them.

Some mud houses are built with mud bricks. You can make mud bricks, too.

What you need
soil

water

straw or grass

large milk carton

What You Do

1. Put two handfuls of soil into a bowl.

2. Add water until the soil becomes thick mud.

3. Add some straw and grass.

4. Cut a large milk carton in half. Pour in the mud.

5. Put the carton in the sun to dry. Wait a couple of days.

6. Pop the mud brick out of the carton.

Adding straw or grass is important because they hold the mud together.

Reflect on

Strategies: What information did you gather by reading the text of this article? What information did you gather from the photos and captions?

Connections: When have you seen animals using mud to build homes or nests?

Investigating Soil

by Tamara Gould

Applying Strategies

Synthesizing

As you read, remember to use the strategy of synthesizing:

- Think about what you already know.

- Gather information from text, visuals, and captions.

- Fit information together to build a new understanding.

Different plants need different types of soil to grow and stay healthy. Most plants in Canada need soil that is dark brown and feels spongy and soft. It also has to have the right amount of clay, silt, and sand.

How do you find out if soil in your neighbourhood is good for most Canadian plants? Do the easy experiment below.

What You Need

- a small shovel

- soil

- a large jar with a lid

- water

With your teacher, collect soil from a park, forest, schoolyard, or beach.

What You Do

1. With your teacher's help, dig up some soil with your shovel.

2. Fill your jar halfway with soil.

3. Add water until the jar is almost full. Screw the lid on tightly.

4. Shake the jar for about 30 seconds. Set the jar down.

5. Let the jar sit overnight and check it in the morning.

water

clay

silt

sand

gravel

The Results

What happened to the soil in the jar? It should have formed into layers.

This diagram shows a sample of soil that would be good for growing most Canadian plants. The soil is separated into layers. It has the same amounts of clay, silt, and sand. This soil is good because it can hold the water that plant roots need.

Soil that has too much sand does not hold water. Soil that has too little sand holds too much water, which may make the plant roots rot.

Compare your jar of soil to the diagram. Do you think most Canadian plants would grow well in your soil?

Reflect on

Strategies: What did you already know about soil before you read this article? What new information did you gather?

Your Learning: What kind of soil do you think is most common in your neighbourhood? Why?

My Desert Home

Applying Strategies

Synthesizing

As you read, remember to use the strategy of synthesizing:

- Think about what you already know.

- Gather information from text, visuals, and captions.

- Fit information together to build a new understanding.

Hi. My name is Ada. I live in the Sahara Desert with my family. Our people, the Tuareg, have lived in the desert for thousands of years. We know all about the desert!

Lots of people think they know what it must be like to live in a desert. Some think deserts are nothing but sand dunes. Other people think plants don't grow in the sandy soil, or animals can't live in the sand. Boy, are they wrong!

Ada's family cooks food over a campfire in the desert.

Sand in the Sahara Desert doesn't have a lot of organic matter. *Organic matter* is the dead plants and animals that make soil rich.

More Than Just Sand Dunes

The Sahara Desert has more rocks than sand, but we do have a lot of sand. One sand dune in the Sahara is as large as France!

One interesting fact about our sandy soil is that it's very salty. Thousands of years ago the Sahara was covered by seawater! Now there's hardly any water at all.

The Sahara Desert has oases, places where underground rivers come close to, or above, the surface. Plants can grow well in the soil of an oasis.

If you pick up a handful of desert sand, you can see seeds from dozens of different plants.

Desert Plants

The Sahara Desert is very hot and dry. So, many plants that grow in Canada will not grow here. But there are different types of plants that will grow in the desert.

Most plants that grow in the desert have long roots. Long roots can reach the water that is far underground. Some plants store water in their stems. Other plants only begin to grow when it rains. Most desert plants have seeds that can live in the soil for years, just waiting for water before they grow.

Desert Animals

Many animals live in my beautiful desert. My family keeps camels, goats, sheep, and donkeys.

Wild animals also live in the desert. These are just a few of the animals that live here: scorpions, lizards, foxes, gerbils, cobras, and other snakes.

Many desert animals, like bugs, snakes, and the sand cat, keep cool by staying underground during the day. The deeper you dig down into the sandy soil, the cooler it is!

My desert is hot, dry, sandy, and beautiful!

Desert mole rats live in burrows deep in the sandy soil. They use their front teeth to dig burrows. For food and water, mole rats eat plants and roots.

Reflect on

Strategies: Think of three pieces of information you can fit together to build a new understanding of deserts.

Critical Literacy: How does Ada describe deserts? Do you think everyone would describe deserts in this way? Explain.

Publishing Reports

When you publish a report, you are getting it ready for readers. Titles, headings, and captions can help readers understand what they are reading.

A title tells readers what the topic is. →

Headings show the main parts of a report. ↗

Captions explain what is in photos or illustrations. →

PERMAFROST—SUPER-COLD SOIL
by Wahid

What Is Permafrost?
Permafrost is ground with a temperature at or below 0 °C for at least two years. The word *permafrost* means "permanently frozen ground." You find permafrost where winters are cold and there isn't much snow to protect the ground. The land in these places is called *tundra*.

This rock willow plant has hairy leaves that help it survive the cold.

How to publish reports:

☑ Use the title to tell your readers what the topic is.

☑ Use headings to show the main parts in your report.

☑ Use captions to explain photos or illustrations.

Creepy Crawly Critters

by Angela Bestos

Many squiggly, slimy, creepy, crawly critters live in the soil beneath your feet. Which of these creepy crawlies do you already know about?

A TRAIL OF SLIME

Picture a snail without a shell. That's a slug. Slugs are moist and sticky. When they move, they leave a slimy trail behind. Slugs love to eat dead leaves and plant roots. Some slugs have up to 27 000 teeth! Slugs eat mostly at night. If you want to see one munching, grab a flashlight, get an adult, and visit a garden.

Many people think slugs are pests. That's because slugs eat the roots, stems, and leaves of vegetables.

Grubs lay eggs in the spring. The eggs hatch a few weeks later.

GRUBBY INSECTS

Have you ever seen a small white worm in soil? It was probably a grub. A grub is the baby form of an insect, such as a June beetle. Grubs like to eat the roots of grass. As they get older, they grow hard shells. The shells break open and the insects fly or run away.

LEAPING SPRINGTAILS

Springtails are tiny—most are small enough to fit inside this letter o. They have six legs. Two bendy feelers are attached to a long body. Springtails use a Y-shaped part under their tail to spring into the air. Springtails are harmless to humans and animals. They can't even bite!

Springtails like moisture. You may find them in your kitchen sink on a dry, hot summer day.

TINY, BUT MIGHTY

Soil mites are tiny in size, but huge in numbers. There are over a million different kinds of soil mites. They don't have eyes, so they move through the soil by touch. The biggest soil mites tear apart insects with their fangs.

FANCY FOOTWORK

Millipedes can have up to 400 legs. They need all those legs to run away from birds, beetles, and other insects that find them tasty to eat. Millipedes like to eat soft, dead plant material. They have trouble chewing through tough plants because their mouths are weak.

Mites are colourful. They can be blue, red, green, or beige.

Millipedes don't like sunlight. They live in the soil under leaves, stones, and logs where it is dark.

Reflect on

Writer's Craft: How did the title, headings, and captions help you understand the article?

Critical Literacy: Do you think the writer of this article would be excited to find one of the creepy crawly critters she writes about? What makes you think so?

How Does Your Garden Grow?

Identifying Conventions of Seed Packages

A package of seeds has almost everything a gardener needs to start a garden. Besides seeds, a seed package has valuable information about planting, types of soil, and fertilization.

**$1.99
50 seeds**

Morgan's Garden Supplies

Petunia Seeds

SINCE 2000

ANNUAL

The front of the seed package shows what the plant will look like. How does this seed package help a gardener decide whether or not to plant the seeds inside?

The back of a seed package often has a chart with facts about the plant. How deeply should you plant these seeds in the soil? How tall will the petunias grow?

Petunia

Annual	Full sun	Plant 3 mm deep	Space seeds 20 cm apart	Grow to 30 cm

The back of a seed package tells you how to plant the seeds. What might happen if these seeds were planted in the shade? What kind of soil is best for these seeds?

Plant indoors in starter pots in early March. Lightly cover seeds with topsoil. Keep pots at 24 °C. When seedlings appear keep at 20 °C. Plant outside after last frost.

For best results, plant in well-drained soil with full sun. Water regularly.

9 780176 238520

Read this package. What do you have to do to grow
the biggest pumpkin?

Giant Atlantic Pumpkins

In small pots indoors, start the seeds 3 to 4 weeks before the last frost is expected. When the ground is warm, plant the seedlings. When the fruits appear, prune all but one or two fruits. Water often and add fertilizer. Pumpkins grow best in rich, moist, well-drained soil with lots of compost.

Pumpkins grow to 45 kg or larger!	Space seeds 1.5 m apart	Plant 2.5 cm deep	Full sun	Annual

Seeds must be started indoors in March.

9 780176 238520 2

Worm Farm

Putting It All Together

As you read, remember to use the strategies you learned in this unit:

- Identify characteristics of question-and-answer text pattern.
- Synthesize.
- Identify the title, headings, and captions.

If we didn't have healthy soil, life on Earth wouldn't exist. So, what can you do to get healthy soil? You can make a worm farm!

What's a worm farm?

A worm farm is a container in which you keep worms and compost (leaves and food scraps). The worms eat the compost and make soil.

How do you make a worm farm?

Find a plastic bin at least 30 cm deep. Find a shady place for it outside. Get an adult to put little holes in the bottom of it. The holes will allow the water to drain out. Gather fallen leaves, soil, and shredded newspaper. (This is the "bedding.") Fill the bin with bedding about halfway. Add water to moisten the bedding. Now put 12 red worms into the bin.

Super Soil

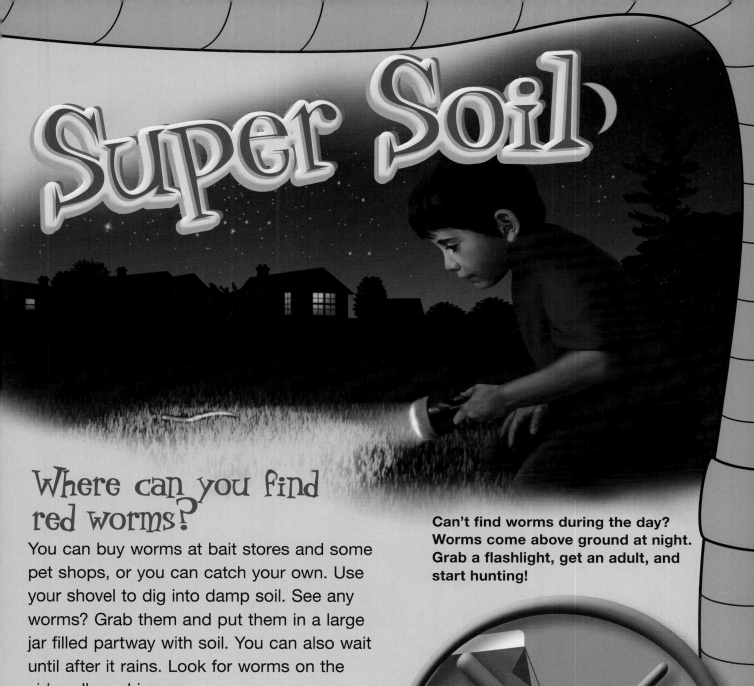

Where can you find red worms?

You can buy worms at bait stores and some pet shops, or you can catch your own. Use your shovel to dig into damp soil. See any worms? Grab them and put them in a large jar filled partway with soil. You can also wait until after it rains. Look for worms on the sidewalk or driveway.

Can't find worms during the day? Worms come above ground at night. Grab a flashlight, get an adult, and start hunting!

What do you feed the worms?

Gather food scraps, such as tea bags, eggshells, fruit and vegetable peels, coffee grounds, and stale bread. Add these scraps to the bin and give the bedding a stir.

MILK

Worms won't eat dairy or meat products. If you add these to the bin, they will go rotten and smell.

What's going on in the worm farm?

Do you see any new worms in the bin? That's good. Add more food scraps. If the bin smells, check for dead worms and remove them.

New soil doesn't happen overnight. It takes worms three to six months to use all the bedding. As the bedding disappears, new soil forms.

What do you do with the new soil?

With your shovel, remove about half of the soil from the bin. Use it for your plants. Then fill the bin back up with new bedding.

Worms eat the bedding.

New worms are born.

Worms mix the bedding together.

Six months later, the new soil is soft, dark, and crumbly. It is perfect for plants.

Reflect on

Strategies: How did the strategies you learned in this unit help you understand what you were reading?

Connections: What part of creating a worm farm do you think would be easy for you? What part might be difficult? Why?

Credits

This page constitutes an extension of the copyright page. We have made every effort to trace the ownership of all copyrighted material and to secure permission from copyright holders. In the event of any question arising as to the use of any material, we will be pleased to make the necessary corrections in future printings. Thanks are due to the following authors, publishers, and agents for permission to use the material indicated.

Photos

Cover: (tortoise and hare) illustrated by Matt Roussel (worm) Konrad Wothe/Minden Pictures/Getty Images (CN Tower) IntraClique /Shutterstock; **5:** © David Wall / Alamy; FoodPix/Jupiter Images **51:** Greg Pease/Photographer's Choice/Getty; **52-53:** (background) Kostas Tsipos/Shutterstock; **52:** (clockwise) © David Wall / Alamy; Andrew Buckin/ Shutterstock; Martine Oger/Shutterstock; **53:** (clockwise) 4736202690/Shutterstock; Margo Harrison/Shutterstock; Jose AS Reyes/Shutterstock; **54:** (top to bottom) I. Kolesnik/ Shutterstock; Lance Bellers/Shutterstock; **55:** (top to bottom) SNEHIT/Shutterstock; Joe Gough/Shutterstock; **56:** (top to bottom) Péter Gudella/Shutterstock; Elena Itsenko/ Shutterstock; Feverpitch/Shutterstock; **57:** (top to bottom) prism_68/Shutterstock; Donna Heatfield/Shutterstock; arway/Shutterstock; Joe Gough/Shutterstock; **58:** Thorsten Milse/ First Light; **59:** (top to bottom) Lorraine Swanson/Shutterstock; inacio pires/Shutterstock; **61:** (top to bottom) Leslie Newman & Andrew Flowers/Photo Researchers, Inc.; © Cephas Picture Library/Alamy; **62:** Sasha Moroz; **64:** Simon Phipps/iStockphoto; **65:** (top to bottom) Coia Hubert/Shutterstock; Peggy Easterly/Shutterstock; **66:** Joseph DiGrazia/ Shutterstock; **67:** 3483253554/Shutterstock; **68:** R. S. Ryan/Shutterstock; **69:** photobank. ch/Shutterstock; **71-72:** (background) prism_68/Shutterstock; (pins) Pepita/Shutterstock; **71:** V. J. Matthew/Shutterstock; Supreme Graphics/Shutterstock; **72:** KAKABA/Shutterstock; © James Leynse/Corbis; **73:** © infocusphotos.com/Alamy; **76:** ©Werner Forman/Topham/ The Image Works; Florin Cirstoc/Shutterstock; **77:** © nagelestock.com/Alamy; **80-82:** sabri deniz kizil/Shutterstock; **83:** Sasha Moroz; **84-88:** (background) Luther/Shutterstock; **84:** Thomas Sztanek/Shutterstock; **86:** (top to bottom) David McNew/Getty Images; Linda Bucklin/Shutterstock; **87:** John Russell/Photonica/Getty Images; **88:** (left to right) Tan Kian Khoon/Shutterstock; Christophe Namur/Shutterstock **89:** (clockwise) Olivier Le Queinec / Shutterstock © Martin Meyer/zefa/Corbis; **92-95:** (background, top to bottom) Katerina Havelkova/Shutterstock; Nanka (Kucherenko Olena)/Shutterstock; Photodisc Photography/ Veer; **92-93:** MANDY GODBEHEAR/Shutterstock; **93:** Steve Baccon/Digital Vision/Getty Images; **95:** (left to right) photoalto/First Light; Nanka (Kucherenko Olena)/Shutterstock; letty17/Shutterstock; **96–98:** Good Mood Photo/Shutterstock; **96:** Kenneth H. Thomas/ Photoresearchers/First Light; **97:** Gladkova Svetlana/Shutterstock; **98:** © Corbis; **99:** © neil hardwick / Alamy; **100:** Eastcott Momatiuk/Photodisc/Getty Images; Paul J. Fusco/ Photoresearchers/First Light; **101:** © Mikephotos | Dreamstime.com; Heinrich van den Berg/Gallo Images/Getty Images; **102:** © Garth McElroy/Visuals Unlimited, Inc.; **104-107:** (background) fotoar/Shutterstock; **104:** Nigel Cattlin/Visuals Unlimited, Inc.; **105:** © Papilio/ Alamy; **106:** (top to bottom) Kathie Atkinson/Oxford Scientific/Jupiter Images; matthew palmer/iStockphoto; **107:** (top to bottom)Dusty Cline/Shutterstock; FoodPix/Jupiter Images; **108:** Andrea Booher/Stone/Getty Images; **109:** © imagebroker/Alamy; **110:** Daniel Mihailescu/AFP/Getty Images; **111:** Sasha Moroz; **113:** Sasha Moroz; **114:** (top to bottom) Dmytro Korolov/Shutterstock; Frans Lemmens/Photographer's Choice/Getty Images; **114-117:** (background) sylvaine thomas/Shutterstock; **115:** Regien Paassen/Shutterstock; **116:** (top to bottom) Frank Krahmer/IFA Bilderteam/Jupiter Images; Dmitry Rukhlenko/

Illustrations

Text